SPIRIT TO SPIRIT

"What the Lord told me- Spirit to Spirit"

Lessons of life: love, happiness and the power of The Holy Spirit

ISBN# 0983075123

P. O. Box 437155

Chicago, IL. 60643

773-568-2274

Email: sharonpcarson@gmail.com

DEDICATION

To my Children: John, Mark & Tracy

Colossians 2:2-3 (New Living Translation)

[2] I want them to be encouraged and knit together by strong ties of love. I want them to have complete confidence that they understand God's mysterious plan, which is Christ himself. [3] In him lies all the hidden treasures of wisdom and knowledge.

Table of Contents

INTRODUCTION 1

HE CHOSE YOU 5

YOUR LIFE HAS PURPOSES – YES WITH AN "S" 8

THE UNNEIGHBORLY NEIGHBOR 10

YOUR ARE NOT AT RISK 12

THE PERFECT MARRIAGE MYTH 14

CHANGE YOUR MIND 15

HOUSE HUNTING WITH THE LORD 16

DO YOU QUALIFY FOR EXEMPTION? 18

GOD'S SOFTWARE FOR CHILDREN 19

WHAT CHILDREN NEED TO KNOW 21

LET YOUR HEART DO THE TALKING 23

MELTING IN GOD'S LOVE 24

THE GREATEST LOVE 25

THE CHOICE IS THEIRS 27

THE DIVINE BABY SITTER 28

PONDER THIS 29

THE JOY STEALER 30

FEEL YOUR FAITH 32

YOU ARE MORE THAN A HOUSE FLY 34

THE EYES OF THE TRUE BEHOLDER 35

NO FOR SALE SIGNS IN HEAVEN 36

THE LARGEST STONE IN THE CEMETARY 37

THE PRICE OF A DAY 39

LOVING THE UNLOVABLE 40

WHAT? NO LOBSTER IN HEAVEN............................. 41

THE HOLY SPIRIT 42

RUSHING PAST LIFE TO GET TO HEAVEN 51

WHY CLIMB A MOUNTAIN WHEN YOU CAN
MOVE IT? 53

ITCHING EARS 55

NO GAMES WITH GOD... 59

FISHING AROUND WITH PROBLEMS 60

GOD SAID IT AND WE CAN SEE IT............................... 61

THE ONE ROAD MAP.. 63

COMMUNICATE WITH YOUR BODY 64

RESISTING TEMPTATION.. 66

THE LIFE CHANGER 67

FILL THE GAP 68

GOD CAN MULTI-TASK 70

TIME TELLS THE TRUTH.. 72

WINDOWS OF THE MIND 73

THE CLEANSING 75

WORRY IS A BAD DINNER DATE 76

WORK TO LIVE NOT TO WORK 77

THE GRUDGE HOLDER.. 79

UNHAPPY BIRTHDAYS.. 80

WE NEVER GET CLOSE TO PERFECT 82

SIP YOUR LIFE 83

COLLECT YOUR INHERITANCE 84

WHAT'S THE DIFFERENCE? 86

THE MARRIAGE MOBILE 87

DEPOSIT INTO YOUR MERCY ACCOUNT 89

SHOW HIM AND HE WILL SHOW YOU 90

TWO THINGS GOD TOLD ME NEVER TO FORGET .. 91

FOR ONE THING OR ANOTHER 93

THE RULES OF GOD'S ROAD 94

HOME SCHOOLING 96

GOD'S BABY SHOWER 98

KEEP YOUR GPS ON (GOD'S POSITIONING
SYSTEM) 100

THE SIMPLICITY OF SALVATION 101

LONG DISTANCE LOVING 103

MEASURING SUCCESS 104

GOD DOES NOT WANT YOU TO BE POOR 105

PERCEPTION 107

SEEING IS NOT BELIEVING 108

TELL THE TRUTH BUT… 109

LESSONS OF LIFE 110

NO VIPS WITH GOD 111

THE TONGUE FIGHT 112

HEALING OR REVEALING 113

GOD HEARD YOU BEFORE YOU 114

THE DIVINE RECIPE FOR EVERYTHING 116

FRIENDS FOR A REASON AND A SEASON 118

LOVE YOUR NEIGHBOR BUT DON'T FORGET
YOURSELF 119

LIFE HAS MANY TEACHERS 121

WHOM WOULD YOU NOT WANT TO SEE IN
HEAVEN? 122

THE REPETITIOUS PRAYER 123

HOW? WHEN? WHAT? WHERE? GOD 125

THE THOUGHT THIEF 126

TIT FOR TAT 127

WHAT GOD WILL NOT REMEMBER 128

ANOTHER WAY TO LOOK AT IT 129

THE EMOTIONS CONTROLLER 130

THE ULTIMATE LACK OF FAITH 132

UNMERITED FAVOR 135

NAME YOUR OWN HOLIDAY 137

YOU HAVE WHAT YOU NEED TO GET WHAT
YOU WANT 138

FOLLOWING THE LEADER 140

FROM FOE TO FRIEND 141

WHEN GOD SAYS NO 142

NO COMPARISON 144

GET OUT OF LIFE ALIVE 145

HOLIER THAN THOU 146

THE SALUTATION TO LIFE 148

YOU, THE LIFE CHANGER 149

THE HEALER 150

DON'T LOSE YOURSELF... 151

FAMILY AFFAIRS.. 152

DON'T BE CHOSEN 153

DON'T MAKE A U-TURN 154

HEART TO HEART.. 156

THE SCHOOL OF LIFE 157

THE MARRIAGE REHEARSAL 159

THE PLEASER 161

THE POWER WORD.. 162

THE HAPPINESS KEEPER 163

INTRODUCTION

There is one thing I know beyond a shadow of any doubt, and that is God desires to converse with his children. But to do so, he needs us to be able to recognize his voice as he speaks to our spirit.

Most of us don't have any problem communicating our thoughts and problems to God but our inability to recognize his voice as he speaks back to us to provide us with the wisdom and direction; we need to travel on the divine path of our lives.

God is God and he has the power to speak by any means he chooses, including audibly but if he chose to speak audibly the deaf would not hear him. God is a spirit and he speaks spirit to spirit in his unmistakable voice.

He speaks in a soft calm voice that can be heard loudly when you tune out everything but him. He is God and he will neither shout to be heard nor compete for your attention.

If you ask God to respond to you with wisdom, direction and answers for your problems, you must await his timely response with faithful expectation. His answers will always come on time and in due time, and it is important for you not to move ahead of his direction. When you move ahead of him without clear direction from him, you are moving in the wrong direction.

When God speaks to your spirit he will never speak anything that is contrary to his written word in the Bible.

You will have confidence in his response and his direction because it will be accompanied by his peace. You will know that you know that you know that you have heard the unmistakable voice of the living God.

I have often said to God; "Speak to me Lord, speak profoundly to my spirit and let me know that it is you that is speaking and not my own limited intellect".

Sometimes God would ask; "what do you want me to speak to you about"? And I would ask him to speak concerning something specific that was going on in my life or I would ask him to just speak some wisdom to me of his choosing.

However long it took, seconds, minutes or longer God would always speak. He would speak so profoundly about what I had asked him to speak about or provide so much new awesome wisdom that I knew within my spirit that it was God and my response would often be; "Wow! God that was awesome".

I cannot adequately describe in words, the experience and feeling I get from hearing God speaks. It is something that you have to experience for yourself to truly understand it and it is an experience that is available to you every second of every day of your life.

Once you have learned to hear the voice of God, conversations with him will become as natural as breathing. Conversations with God will provide you with all the wisdom, answers and direction you need for a life that is filled with love, peace, joy and abundance of blessings which is the life that God desires for his children.

Through the death, burial and resurrection of our intercessor and Savior Jesus Christ, we have been provided eternal access to God and we can talk directly to him. But to experience the totality of the salvation that Jesus has provided, we must not only speak to God, we must learn to hear God speak to us.

God is always online, never has an away message, never sends you into voice mail and never refers you to an angel to take a message.

All that is written in this book is based on my personal conversations with God and embody the essence of what the Lord told me SPIRIT TO SPIRIT

HE CHOSE YOU

A woman is born with over a million egg cells stored in her ovaries. And if God had wanted to, He could have designed her to embody an infinite supply of what we can call human possibilities.

God is the giver of life, and He gives it not to those who would be perfect, because there are none, but to those who are perfect for His divine purposes.

I had often wondered why God called me into life out of all of my potential brothers and sisters.

Then one day God revealed to me that I was selected not only for His earthly purposes but for a higher heavenly purpose.

God wanted to provide me with the opportunity to spend eternity with Him in His paradise of heaven.

Yes, He chose me knowing everything about me before I was born. He wasn't surprised by my personality, level of intelligence, education, outer appearance, sex, or my ethnicity.

He knew every thought I would think, mistake I would make and sins I would commit.

He knew my name and called me by my name to come forth to life, just as he called Lazareth to come forth from death.

Just as God has chosen me, He has also chosen you; and you should know that:

You are who God knew you would be and more than you think you are!

John 15:16 (King James Version)

[16]Ye have not chosen me, but I have chosen you, and ordained you, that ye should go and bring forth fruit, and that your fruit should remain: that whatsoever ye shall ask of the Father in my name, he may give it you.

Ephesians 1:4 (King James Version)

[4]According as he hath chosen us in him before the foundation of the world

Jeremiah 1:5 (King James Version)

⁵Before I formed thee in the belly I knew thee

Psalm 139:16 (King James Version)

¹⁶Thine eyes did see my substance, yet being unperfect; and in thy book all my members were written, which in continuance were fashioned, when as yet there was none of them.

YOUR LIFE HAS PURPOSES – YES
WITH AN "S"

God has divine purposes for everything He created.

If, however we had only one purpose and we fulfilled it on yesterday, would the remainder of our life have any divine purpose?

God is not wasteful; there is divine purpose in every day of our lives. No matter how large or small what we do may seem to us or to others, the sum of our lives, divine daily purposes is our divine purpose.

Although we may never know all of our many purposes,   we can fulfill them by living lives that are lead by love. Love is the guiding light to our purposes because God is the guide, and God is Love.

1 John 4:8 (King James Version)

[8]He that loveth not knoweth not God; for God is love

Proverbs 16:4 (New Living Translation)

[4] The LORD has made everything for his own purposes,

Philippians 2:13 (King James Version)

[13]For it is God which worketh in you both to will and to do of his good pleasure.

THE UNNEIGHBORLY NEIGHBOR

One of my neighbor's young sons who was involved in illegal activity was a real problem for my community.

One day, I prayed to the Lord that He would move this young man out of the community or have him arrested, and sent to jail as a consequence of all the illegal activity he was involved in.

After that prayer, the Lord spoke the following to my heart, "You have a son who is nearly the same age as the neighbor's son, and if it were your son doing these things, what would your prayer be?"

I then said my prayer would be to save him, Lord; deliver him, Lord; and lead him in the proper path. Have mercy on him, Lord and gently help him to change his ways and become the man you want him to become.

I immediately realized that while the activity of this young man was deserving of arrest and imprisonment as punishment, my only prayer for him was for punishment.

I had never prayed and asked God to save him and change his life. Well, as you can imagine, I stopped praying that way for the other young man and began to pray for him as I would have prayed for my own son. Years later, I ran into the young man and found that God had answered my prayers for him.

Matthew 5:44 (King James Version)

44But I say unto you, Love your enemies, bless them that curse you, do good to them that hate you, and pray for them which despitefully use you, and persecute you;

Romans 13:10 (King James Version)

10Love worketh no ill to his neighbor: therefore love is the fulfilling of the law.

YOUR ARE NOT AT RISK

By examining a patient's family medical history, physicians try to determine if there is an increased risk of the patient developing a particular disease or inherited condition.

From a spiritual perspective, however, Christians are part of the family of God, their father God, his Son Jesus, and The Holy Spirit; and there is neither sickness nor disease in the history of this family, and there never will be.

When Jesus died on the cross, He took upon Himself as a vaccination, all sickness and disease known and unknown to man and provided us with immunity from them. We as Christians are not, therefore, at risk for any sickness or disease.

Ephesians 2:19 (New Living Translation)

[19] So now you Gentiles are no longer strangers and foreigners. You are citizens along with all of God's holy people. You are members of God's family.

Matthew 8:17 (New Living Translation)

[17] This fulfilled the word of the Lord through the prophet Isaiah, who said,

"He took our sicknesses
and removed our diseases."[a]

Psalm 91:9-10 (King James Version)

[9]Because thou hast made the LORD, which is my refuge, even the most High, thy habitation;

[10]There shall no evil befall thee, neither shall any plague come nigh thy dwelling.

THE PERFECT MARRIAGE MYTH

Couples should not compare their marriages to that of another couple.

There are no perfect marriages because there are no two perfect people   who can be put together to make one.

A strong marriage, however, that can stand the test of time can be built upon a foundation of communication, commitment, compromise and Christ.

Ephesians 5:33 (King James Version)

Let every one of you in particular so love his wife even as himself; and the wife see that she reverence her husband

CHANGE YOUR MIND

Rather than dwell on the sadness of what you've been through, rest your thoughts on how wonderful it is that you got through that sadness!

Philippians 4:8 (New King James Version)
⁸ Finally, brethren, whatever things are true, whatever things *are* noble, whatever things *are* just, whatever things *are* pure, whatever things *are* lovely, whatever things *are* of good report, if *there is* any virtue and if *there is* anything praiseworthy—meditate on these things.

HOUSE HUNTING WITH THE LORD

It is important to consult the Lord about where you should live.

You may fall in love with what you can see and may know the neighborhood, but God knows the hearts of your neighbors.

He knows the friends you and your children will meet in the neighborhood and what their influences will be.

You may know that you will have good expressway access, but God knows who and what situations you will encounter on those expressways. While you are looking at the total price of a home, God sees the total picture. He is the best real estate agent ever and He will lead you to the best place for you to live when you consult Him every step of the way.

And you will know when you have found that place by the peace that will accompany your decision to move there. This is God's way of letting you know that you are making a decision that is within his will for you.

Proverbs 3:5-7 (King James Version)

[5]Trust in the LORD with all thine heart; and lean not unto thine own understanding. [6]In all thy ways acknowledge him, and he shall direct thy path.

Philippians 4:7 (King James Version)

[7]And the peace of God, which passeth all understanding, shall keep your hearts and minds through Christ Jesus.

DO YOU QUALIFY FOR EXEMPTION?

Perfect people are the only ones who should have the right not to have to forgive imperfect people.

John 8:7 (New Living Translation)

7 They kept demanding an answer, so he stood up again and said, "All right, but let the one who has never sinned throw the first stone!"

Romans 3:23 (King James Version)

23For all have sinned, and come short of the glory of God;

Matthew 6:15 (King James Version)

15But if ye forgive not men their trespasses, neither will your Father forgive your trespasses

GOD'S SOFTWARE FOR CHILDREN

Our children are given to us as gifts from God. They come to us like a newly manufactured computer with no installed software.

Parents are given the responsibility of installing the right programs in their children, and the most important program they need is not Microsoft Word but rather "The word of God".

Parents should install this program in their children and pray that it will remain saved in the hard drives of their minds and spirits and that they will have enough memory to allow it to work throughout their lives because at some point parents will have to click RUN and let their children go.

Proverbs 22:6 (King James Version)

[6]Train up a child in the way he should go: and when he is old, he will not depart from it.

2 Timothy 3:16-17 (King James Version)

¹⁶All scripture is given by inspiration of God, and is profitable for doctrine, for reproof, for correction, for instruction in righteousness:

¹⁷That the man of God may be perfect, thoroughly furnished unto all good work

WHAT CHILDREN NEED TO KNOW

If our children have been taught by the best schools in the world but have not been taught about God and his unconditional and sacrificial love for them, they have been taught nothing in comparison.

When they are out of our reach or even within our reach, they need to know that they can always reach an almighty God in times of trouble. When the world puts them down, they need to know that God can lift them up. When they are rejected, they need to know that God loves and accepts them unconditionally.

Given the pressures and temptations that they will face in schools and life in general, they need to know that their self-esteem should not be rooted in how others see them but in how God sees them, and He sees them as His perfect creation.

They need to know that God is love; He loves them unconditionally and He is omniscient, omnipotent and omnipresent. They need to know that He has the will and the power to help them at any time, in any place, and in any situation.

Without this knowledge, they are sent into a world at war without the weapons they need for the battles of life.

Isaiah 54:13 (King James Version)

[13]And all thy children shall be taught of the LORD; and great shall be the peace of thy children.

LET YOUR HEART DO THE TALKING

In prayer, it is more important for your heart to be right than for your words to be right. God hears the voice of the heart more than the words of the mouth.

Jeremiah 29:13 (King James Version)

[13]And ye shall seek me, and find me, when ye shall search for me with all your heart.

James 5:16 (New Living Translation)

[16] The earnest prayer of a righteous person has great power and produces wonderful results.

MELTING IN GOD'S LOVE

I was blessed to have had what I believe was an out of body spiritual experience that placed me in the presence of Jesus.

In His presence, I felt so much love that it was as though I was melting in love, which is the only way I can describe it .

This was a profound experience for me, and afterwards, I knew that even with this overwhelming feeling of melting in love, I was only experiencing as much love as I could handle at that moment.

I am now convinced that it is impossible in this human body to feel the totality of God's love. It is only when we get to heaven and have been transformed that we will be able to feel the depth, breath and height of God's love for us because we as humans can love and feel love, but God is love.

Ephesians 3:19 (New Living Translation)

[19] May you experience the love of Christ, though it is too great to understand fully.

THE GREATEST LOVE

Replace the word whosoever in the Bible scripture below (John 3:16) with the name of your worst enemy, if you have one, or a person in history or the news whether dead or alive who has committed one of the worst crimes you have ever read or heard about.

After replacing the word "whosoever" with the name of that person, ask yourself if you would send your only son who was perfect and sinless to suffer a death by crucifixion so that person could have an everlasting life in paradise with God. By doing this, you may have a more profound understanding of God's love for every human being ever born into the world.

If you cannot think of a name to replace "whosoever" with, place the word "whosoever" back in the scripture, and you will realize that it covers everyone.

John 3:16

For God so loved the world, that he gave his only begotten Son, that (whosoever)

_____ believeth in him should not perish, but have everlasting life

1 Peter 3:18 (King James Version)

[18]For Christ also hath once suffered for sins, the just for the unjust, that he might bring us to God, being put to death in the flesh, but quickened by the Spirit:

Romans 5:6 (King James Version)

[6]For when we were yet without strength, in due time Christ died for the ungodly

John 15:13 (King James Version)

[13]Greater love hath no man than this that a man lay down his life for his friends

THE CHOICE IS THEIRS

God told me that as my children become adults, I should not expect them to take a life path of my choice rather than one of their choosing.

They have a right to choose their own sinless paths, and I should not expect them to take a path that would make them unhappy by asking them to take a path that I think would make me happy.

Proverbs 19:21 (Amplified Bible)

[21]Many plans are in a man's mind, but it is the Lord's purpose for him that will stand.

THE DIVINE BABY SITTER

My husband and I were going on vacation, and I asked the Lord to please take care of my children while we were gone. The Lord quickly answered back and said, "Who do you think is taking care of them while you are here?"

2 Timothy 1:12 (American Standard Version)

12   I am persuaded that he is able to guard that which I have committed unto him against that day.

Psalm 127:1 (King James Version)

1Except the LORD builds the house, they labour in vain that build it: except the LORD keep the city, the watchman waketh but in vain.

PONDER THIS

Let the one who can dance ponder the thoughts of the one in a wheel chair, let the one who can sing a song ponder the thoughts of the mute, let the one who can see the sun rise and set ponder the thoughts of the blind and let the one who can hear the words "I love you" ponder the thoughts of those who are deaf.

It is within the depth of these ponderings that one can find reasons to be thankful to God.

Psalm 100:4 (King James Version)

4Enter into his gates with thanksgiving, and into his courts with praise: be thankful unto him, and bless his name

THE JOY STEALER

The devil knows that he cannot stop God from blessing us, so he tries to take our minds off the blessing and find negativity in related things to keep us stressing.

For instance, If God blesses us with a house, the devil will try to get us stressed about the upkeep. If God's blessing is a good job, the devil will try to keep us focused on problems with the coworkers and supervisor. If he gives us a car, the devil wants us stressed about the price of gas.

The devil couldn't take the toy so he tries the next best thing, which is to steal the joy.

John 10:10 (King James Version)

[10]The thief cometh not, but for to steal, and to kill, and to destroy: I am come that they might have life, and that they might have it more abundantly.

2 Corinthians 2:11 (King James Version)

[11]Lest Satan should get an advantage of us: for we are not ignorant of his devices.

FEEL YOUR FAITH

God told me that I should be able to feel my faith.

He said that I should be able to feel my faith just as one feels his fears.

Since feelings of fear produce a spirit of sadness, worry, stress, depression, anxiety, confusion and sickness, then the feeling of faith should produce a spirit of joy, peace, happiness, confidence, tranquility and good health, all feelings that are opposites of what the feelings that fear produces.

1 John 4:18 (King James Version)

[18]There is no fear in love; but perfect love casteth out fear: because fear hath torment. He that feareth is not made perfect in love.

Galatians 5:22 (King James Version)

[22]But the fruit of the Spirit is love, joy, peace, longsuffering, gentleness, goodness, faith,

2 Timothy 1:7 (King James Version)

[7]For God hath not given us the spirit of fear; but of power, and of love, and of a sound mind.

YOU ARE MORE THAN A HOUSE FLY

Whenever the pressures of life begin to challenge your faith in God, you should remind yourself of how much God loves and cares for everything he created, and mankind is his highest creation.

Some animals are not good fighters, but God created them so that they could run fast. How many birds can you find lying on the ground that have died of starvation? He even made the nagging house fly hard for us to catch and destroy.

If God takes care of a house fly, what will he do for you?

Matthew 6: 26 (King James Version)

[26]Behold the fowls of the air: for they sow not, neither do they reap, nor gather into barns; yet your heavenly Father feedeth them. Are ye not much better than they?

THE EYES OF THE TRUE BEHOLDER

Look at the sunrise, the sunset, the stars, the oceans, the flowers and how beautiful they all are. Everything God created is beautiful in His eyes, and since He created us in His own image and likeness, we most certainly are beautiful to Him.

It has been said that beauty is in the eye of the beholder, but the most important beholder to us should be God our creator.

People make their selective judgments of beauty, but God has beheld all of us as beautiful; and we should see ourselves through the eyes of God and not those of people.

Genesis 1:31 (King James Version)

[31]And God saw every thing that he had made, and, behold, it was very good

NO FOR SALE SIGNS IN HEAVEN

God is not counting your tithes and offerings to see if you have paid enough over the years to buy one of His heavenly mansions because none of them are for sale. Salvation is a free gift of God. Rather than counting your tithes and offerings, God is counting the love in your heart.

1 Corinthians 13

[1] If I could speak all the languages of earth and of angels, but didn't love others, I would only be a noisy gong or a clanging cymbal. [2] If I had the gift of prophecy, and if I understood all of God's secret plans and possessed all knowledge, and if I had such faith that I could move mountains, but didn't love others, I would be nothing. [3] If I gave everything I have to the poor and even sacrificed my body, I could boast about it;[a] but if I didn't love others, I would have gained nothing.

THE LARGEST STONE IN THE CEMETARY

One day, I was driving past a cemetery, and I took notice of the huge gravestones as compared with some of the smaller ones, and God spoke to me and asked, "Does it matter who has the largest stone in the cemetery?"

I knew that God was letting me know that He was not concerned with the amount of money a person had before he died; rather, He was concerned with the amount of love a person had in his heart while he was living.

1 Timothy 6:17-19 (King James Version)

[17]Charge them that are rich in this world, that they be not high-minded, nor trust in uncertain riches, but in the living God, who giveth us richly all things to enjoy;

[18]That they do good, that they be rich in good works, ready to distribute, willing to communicate;

[19]Laying up in store for themselves a good foundation against the time to come, that they may lay hold on eternal life.

Psalm 49-16-17 (King James Version)

[16]Be not thou afraid when one is made rich, when the glory of his house is increased;

[17]For when he dieth he shall carry nothing away: his glory shall not descend after him.

THE PRICE OF A DAY

One extra day of life could not be purchased with a collective combination of the value of all the currencies of the world.

Every day of life is priceless and a treasure not to be endured but to be enjoyed!

Psalm 118:24 (King James Version)

[24]This is the day which the LORD hath made; we will rejoice and be glad in it.

LOVING THE UNLOVABLE

The only way to love people who are considered unlovable is to love them the way God loves us. Love them unconditionally and pray for God to deal with their conditions. We as Christians can love a person even though we may not like the person they are.

Matthew 5:46 (King James Version)

46For if ye love them which love you, what reward have ye? do not even the publicans the same?

WHAT?   NO LOBSTER IN HEAVEN

Some might wonder what heaven will be like, if it may be lacking in all of the earthly things we have come to enjoy.

We must remember that everything that has been created on earth was in the mind of God before the mind of man.

God gave mankind the resources and creative powers to produce   everything that is enjoyed on earth, and we can be certain, therefore, that his provisions for us in heaven must be unimaginably more awesome and wonderful for lack of more descriptive words!

1 Corinthians 2:9 (King James Version)

⁹But as it is written: Eye hath not seen, nor ear heard, neither have entered into the heart of man, the things which God hath prepared for them that love him

Hebrews 3:4 (King James Version)

⁴For every house is builded by some man; but he that built all things is God.

THE HOLY SPIRIT

The most life changing conversation that I have ever had with God was concerning The Holy Spirit.

One day, God spoke to my heart that I had a misconception of The Holy Spirit, and I needed know the truth.

All I knew up to that point was that there was something called The Holy Spirit. In the churches that I frequented, it was more commonly and interchangeably called The Holy Ghost.

Some people in church would dance, run around, faint, move uncontrollably or speak in utterances that were not understandable; and it was said that they had the Holy Ghost.

God told me that I needed to study the Bible again with a focus on the Holy Spirit and that The Holy Spirit would teach me about Himself. He told me later that the world is trying to reduce him to a dance.

I went back to the Bible as God had instructed and read scriptures that I had read many times before that referenced The Holy Spirit.

This time, however, as I was reading, God was giving me a greater contextual understanding of The Holy Spirit in scripture.

I learned that God is the Father, the Son and the Holy Spirit!

The Holy Spirit is referenced in the Bible profoundly from Genesis through Revelations because he is an inseparable part of the trinity of God.

THE HOLY SPIRIT REFERENCED IN GENESIS

Genesis 1:1-2 (New King James Version)

¹ In the beginning God created the heavens and the earth. ² The earth was without form, and void; and darkness was[a] on the face of the deep. And the *Spirit of God* was hovering over the face of the waters.

THE HOLY SPIRIT REFERENCED IN REVELATION

Revelation2:7 (New King James Version)

⁷ "He who has an ear, let him hear what *the Spirit* says to the churches. To him who

overcomes I will give to eat from the tree of life, which is in the midst of the Paradise of God"

Mary conceived Jesus by the power of the Holy Ghost

Luke 1:35 (King James Version)

[35] And the angel answered and said unto her, <u>The Holy Ghost</u> shall come upon thee, and the power of the Highest shall overshadow thee: therefore also that holy thing which shall be born of thee shall be called the Son of God.

Jesus arose from the dead by the power of the Holy Spirit

Romans 8:11 (King James Version)

[11]But if <u>the Spirit</u> of him that raised up Jesus from the dead dwell in you, he that raised up Christ from the dead shall also quicken your mortal bodies by <u>his Spirit</u> that dwelleth in you.

Jesus said God would send us the Holy Spirit after his death

John 14:16-17 (King James Version)

[16]And I will pray the Father, and he shall give you another Comforter, that he may abide with you for ever;

[17]Even <u>the Spirit of truth</u>; whom the world cannot receive, because it seeth him not, neither knoweth him: but ye know him; for he dwelleth with you, and shall be in you.

.John 14:26 John 14:26 (King James Version)

[26]*But the Comforter, which is the <u>Holy Ghost</u>, whom the Father will send in my name, he shall teach you all things, and bring all things to your remembrance, whatsoever I have said unto you.*

After Jesus died on the cross, he released the Holy Spirit

Matthew 27:50 (New King James Version)

[50] And Jesus cried out again with a loud voice, and yielded up His spirit.

The disciples received the Holy Spirit

Acts 2:1-4 (King James Version)

[1]And when the day of Pentecost was fully come, they were all with one accord in one place.

²And suddenly there came a sound from heaven as of a rushing mighty wind, and it filled the entire house where they were sitting.

³And there appeared unto them cloven tongues like as of fire, and it sat upon each of them.

⁴And they were all filled with the Holy Ghost, and began to speak with other tongues, as the Spirit gave them utterance.

The Holy Spirit is ours for the asking

Luke 11:13 (New King James Version)

¹³ If you then, being evil, know how to give good gifts to your children, how much more will *your* heavenly Father give the Holy Spirit to those who ask Him!"

Our Body is the home of The Holy Spirit

1 Corinthians 6:19-20 (New King James Version)

¹⁹ Or do you not know that your body is the temple of the Holy Spirit *who is* in you, whom you have from God, and you are not your own? ²⁰ For you were bought at a price; therefore glorify God in your body[a] and in your spirit, which are God's

With the Holy Spirit comes fruit

(Godly character qualities of those filled with the Holy Spirit)

Galatians 5:22-23 (New King James Version)

[22] But the fruit of the Spirit is love, joy, peace, longsuffering, kindness, goodness, faithfulness, [23] gentleness, self-control

The Holy Spirit gives us gifts

1 Corinthians 12:7-11 (King James Version)

[7]But the manifestation of the Spirit is given to every man to profit withal.

[8]For to one is given by the Spirit the word of wisdom; to another the word of knowledge by the same Spirit;

[9]To another faith by the same Spirit; to another the gifts of healing by the same Spirit;

[10]To another working of miracles; to another prophecy; to another discerning of spirits; to another divers kinds of tongues; to another the interpretation of tongues:

[11]But all these worketh that one and the selfsame Spirit, dividing to every man severally as he will.

The Holy Spirit gives us Power

Acts 1:8 (King James Version)

[8]But ye shall receive power, after that the Holy Ghost is come upon you: and ye shall be witnesses unto me both in Jerusalem, and in all Judaea, and in Samaria, and unto the uttermost part of the earth

John 14:12 (King James Version)

[12]Verily, verily, I say unto you, He that believeth on me, the works that I do shall he do also; and greater works than these shall he do; because I go unto my Father.

THE HOLY SPIRIT IS KNOCKING AT YOUR DOOR

Revelation 3:20 (King James Version)

[20]*Behold, I stand at the door, and knock: if any man hear my voice, and open the door, I will come in to him, and will sup with him, and he with me.*

God told me that the preaching of The Holy Spirit is lacking in many churches today and missing in others. Itching ears are causing many to preach what the congregation wants to hear more than what God wants them to hear. God quoted this verse of scripture to me:

Hosea 4:6 (King James Version)

> [6]My people are destroyed for lack of knowledge:

God said that all that The Holy Spirit provides is desperately needed in the world today by many hurting and suffering people who are seeking answers in all of the wrong places and from all the wrong sources.

The Holy Spirit is ours for the asking and He is:

Omnipresent – Everywhere and is there for us whenever we need him.

Omniscient – All-knowing, and knows the present, past and the future, and can lead us and guide us victoriously through all of life's experiences onto eternal life.

Omnipotent – All powerful, and we can access His power to do God's will and to execute His gifts that not only serve us but can serve and help others as well.

God has given us The Holy Spirit not just for the knowing of Him or the preaching about Him but for the demonstration of His power through our faith in that power.

It was best said by the Apostle Paul in *1 Corinthians 2:4-5*

1 Corinthians 2:4-5 (King James Version)

[4]And my speech and my preaching was not with enticing words of man's wisdom, but in demonstration of the Spirit and of power:

[5]That your faith should not stand in the wisdom of men, but in the power of God

I still have much to learn about The Holy Spirit because The Holy Spirit is a constant and ever present teacher.

What I have learned, however, about The Holy Spirit has been life changing for me.   I know beyond a shadow of a doubt that The Holy Spirit is ours for the asking and that He is a fulfillment of what God said in:

Hebrews 13:5

I will never leave thee, nor forsake thee.

RUSHING PAST LIFE TO GET TO HEAVEN

God promised Christians an eternal life with Him in His paradise of Heaven, and it is natural for us with all of our earthly challenges to long to get there.

God, however, does not want our longing for heaven to cause us to belittle his gift of life.

God wants us to live a long, blessed life on earth and then continue on to His promised reward of eternal life in heaven.

Just as Salvation gifted from the death, burial and resurrection of Jesus Christ has provided us with eternal life. It has also provided us with an abundant and victorious life here on earth.

If we can trust God for his promise of blessings awaiting us in heaven, we should be able to trust Him to give us the blessings He promised for our lifetime here on earth as well.

Romans 8:32 (King James Version)

51

[32]He that spared not his own Son, but delivered him up for us all, how shall he not with him also freely give us all things?

John 10:10 (King James Version)

[10]The thief cometh not, but for to steal, and to kill, and to destroy: I am come that they might have life, and that they might have it more abundantly

WHY CLIMB A MOUNTAIN WHEN YOU CAN MOVE IT?

Our problems often seem like mountains that we feel incapable of climbing. We should know that God did not create us to be mountain climbers; He created us to be mountain movers.

We need to speak to these mountains of problems with faith and authority and command them to move by the power of The Holy Spirit who lives within us.

The same power that moved the planets, seas and continents into their places dwells in us, and it can most certainly move any mountain of problems that stand in the way of the blessings of God.

Mark 11:23 (King James Version)

[23] "For verily I say unto you, That whosoever shall say unto this mountain, Be thou removed, and be thou cast into the sea; and shall not doubt in his heart, but shall believe that those things which he saith shall come to pass; he shall have whatsoever he saith."

Matthew 17:20 (King James Version)

[20] "And Jesus said unto them, Because of your unbelief: for verily I say unto you, If ye have faith as a grain of mustard seed, ye shall say unto this mountain, Remove hence to yonder place; and it shall remove; and nothing shall be impossible unto you".

ITCHING EARS

Far too many people are seeking answers to their problems from the wrong people, in the wrong places and within wrong doctrines.

The Bible is the true word of God and has the answers to every problem one will ever face in life.

The truths in the Bible, however, are too often twisted, turned around and extracted in part and out of context to produce false doctrines masking themselves as new revelations. This is the New Age doctrine of man that is not of God.

There are many preachers of false doctrines who fear empty seats more than they fear God. They deliver sermons that tell the listeners what they want to hear rather than what God would want them to hear.

The teaching of God's gift of salvation through the shed blood of Jesus Christ and the preaching of the power, gifts and fruit of The Holy Spirit is no longer a priority in many churches today. Many Sunday sermons are inspired more by the Spirit of the congregation than the Spirit of God.

We live at a time when it is considered politically correct for Christians to talk about God but politically incorrect to connect Him with Jesus even when the Bible tells us that they are one.

John 10:30 (New King James Version)

[30] "I and *My* Father are one."

John 14:6 (New King James Version)

[6] Jesus said to him, "I am the way, the truth, and the life. No one comes to the Father except through me

We are living at a time when what God has said is right is called wrong and what God has said is wrong is called acceptable. God will never change His position on any issues to accommodate present day lifestyles and lusts.

God has not changed, and His word has not changed; but false, eloquent and crafty teachers and preachers are manipulating the word of God and are deceiving many people.

And although some may be hard for us to unmask, they cannot fool The Holy Spirit; and as we become one with the spirit of God, The

Holy Spirit will reveal them to us. We must, however, be open to the revealed truth and be willing to follow God rather than man.

2 Timothy 4:3-4 (King James Version)

[3]For the time will come when they will not endure sound doctrine; but after their own lusts shall they heap to themselves teachers, having itching ears;[4]And they shall turn away their ears from the truth, and shall be turned unto fables.

1 John 4:1-4

[1] Beloved, do not believe every spirit, but test the spirits, whether they are of God; because many false prophets have gone out into the world. [2] By this you know the Spirit of God: Every spirit that confesses that Jesus Christ has come in the flesh is of God, [3] and every spirit that does not confess that[a] Jesus Christ has come in the flesh is not of God. And this is the *spirit* of the Antichrist, which you have heard was coming, and is now already in the world.[4] You are of God, little children, and have overcome them, because He who is in you is greater than he who is in the world. [5] They are of the world. Therefore they speak *as* of the world, and the world hears them.

John 14:26 (King James Version)

²⁶But the Comforter, which is the Holy Ghost, whom the Father will send in my name, he shall teach you all things, and bring all things to your remembrance, whatsoever I have said unto you.

Deuteronomy 4:2 (King James Version)

²Ye shall not add unto the word which I command you, neither shall ye diminish ought from it,

Hebrews 13:8 (King James Version)

⁸Jesus Christ the same yesterday, and to day, and for ever.

NO GAMES WITH GOD

God has not challenged us to a game of Hide and Blessings Seek. He has not hidden our blessings and challenged us to blindly seek and find them or live a life of poverty without the abundance that Jesus died for us to have in this lifetime.

God has given us The Holy Spirit, our omniscient guide, to place us on the path of life that leads to our prepared and personalized blessings. All we have to do is ask The Holy Spirit to guide us and then follow His lead.

Matthew 7:7(Kings James Version)

"Ask, and it shall be given you, seek and ye shall find, knock and the door shall be opened unto you.

1 Corinthians 2:11 (King James Version)

[11]For what man knoweth the things of a man, save the spirit of man which is in him? Even so the things of God knoweth no man, but the Spirit of God.

FISHING AROUND WITH PROBLEMS

God always wants us to cast our problems onto Him so that He can take care of them. But we often cast them like a fishing pole that casts them out to God and then pulls them back again.

We should cast our problems onto God as a stone across the ocean with a mindset that never wants them back.

1 Peter 5:7 (King James Version)

[7]Casting all your care upon him; for he careth for you.

GOD SAID IT AND WE CAN SEE IT

In the book of Genesis, the words "God Said" were used before everything that God created, and when God finished in Genesis 1:31, it reads, " And God Saw." By this we know that what God says He will see.

The creative powers of God's words apply not just to God's physical creations but to the creation of all of the promises of God.

Find the promises in God's word that you want to see manifested in your life, and speak the promises out loud with faith in God's word just as God did, and then speak these words out loud "because God said it, I shall see it."

Isaiah 55:11 (King James Version)

[11]So shall my word be that goeth forth out of my mouth: it shall not return unto me void, but it shall accomplish that which I please, and it shall prosper in the thing whereto I sent it.

Mark 11:22:23 (King James Version)

²² And Jesus answering saith unto them, Have faith in God

²³ For verily I say unto you, That whosoever shall say unto this mountain, Be thou removed and be thou cast into the sea; and shall not doubt in his heart, but shall believe that those things which he saith shall come to pass; he shall have whatsoever he saith.

THE ONE ROAD MAP

God has given us a road map to heaven, and there is only one road on the map. God made the map very simple so that no one would have to get lost. Mankind has tried to complicate the road map by adding additional roads, rules of the road, as well as telling us that we must pay a toll when the entire price of our trip to heaven has already been paid for by Jesus.

But the fact remains that on God's road map to heaven, there is only one way and one road, and that road and that way to heaven is named Jesus Christ!

John 14:6 (King James Version)

⁶Jesus saith unto him, I am the way, the truth, and the life: no man cometh unto the Father, but by me.

Romans 10:9 (King James Version)

⁹That if thou shalt confess with thy mouth the Lord Jesus, and shalt believe in thine heart that God hath raised him from the dead, thou shalt be saved

COMMUNICATE WITH YOUR BODY

Your body has its way of communicating with you and letting you know when something is wrong with it, and you should learn to speak back to it.

You should speak to your body when you are healthy as well as when you need healing. Speak to specific organs as well. You should compliment your body on how wonderfully God made it and how important it is for everything in it to function to perfection according to the will of God.

You should remind your body that it is the temple of The Holy Spirit and that it is important for it to remain healthy and energized so that you can continue to fulfill God's purposes for your life.

You have the power to lay hands on your own body and command your body as well as specific organs in the name of Jesus to be healed and to function perfectly, according to the divine design of God. If believers can lay hand on others and see them healed, they can certainly lay hands on themselves and see the same result.

Mark 16:17-18 (King James Version)

[17]And these signs shall follow them that believe; In my name shall they cast out devils; they shall speak with new tongues;

[18]They shall take up serpents; and if they drink any deadly thing, it shall not hurt them; they shall lay hands on the sick, and they shall recover.

Psalm 139:14 (King James Version)

[14]I will praise thee; for I am fearfully and wonderfully made: marvellous are thy works

1 Corinthians 6:19 (King James Version)

19   What? Know ye not that your body is the temple of the Holy Ghost which is in you, which ye have of God, and ye are not your own?

RESISTING TEMPTATION

When your desire to please God becomes stronger than your desire to please yourself, you will be less likely to act upon your temptations

Matthew 26:41 (King James Version)

[41]Watch and pray, that ye enter not into temptation: the spirit indeed is willing, but the flesh is weak.

THE LIFE CHANGER

We may be able to cause a person to change his mind, but God can cause a life-changing change of heart.

Ezekiel 36:26-27 (King James Version)

[26]A new heart also will I give you, and a new spirit will I put within you: and I will take away the stony heart out of your flesh, and I will give you an heart of flesh.

[27]And I will put my spirit within you, and cause you to walk in my statutes, and ye shall keep my judgments, and do them.

FILL THE GAP

Faith in God is the key to happiness.

Stress over unfulfilled needs or desires, whether those of ourselves, our family or others, is the typical cause of unhappiness.

God has promised that he would supply all of our needs as well as our desires; therefore, if we have faith that God will do all that He said He would, we should not be unhappy.

Happiness can be sustained by filling the gap that is between prayer and manifestation with the faithful expectation that God will honor His word.

Hebrews 11:1 (King James Version)

[1]Now faith is the substance of things hoped for, the evidence of things not seen.

Psalm 37:4 (King James Version)

[4]Delight thyself also in the LORD: and he shall give thee the desires of thine heart.

Philippians 4:19 (King James Version)

[19]But my God shall supply all your need according to his riches in glory by Christ Jesus.

Numbers 23:19 (King James Version)

[19]God is not a man, that he should lie; neither the son of man, that he should repent: hath he said, and shall he not do it? or hath he spoken, and shall he not make it good?

GOD CAN MULTI-TASK

For those who would say that God is not concerned with the little problems in our lives, they should know that all of our problems are little to our almighty God

Why, therefore, should we say to God, "You handle the big problems, and I will handle the little ones."

Why should we to try to measure the difficulty of our problems to determine which ones to give to God when he has asked for all of them?

God cares about everything we care about, and there is no care of ours that can ever be too large or small for Him to take care of.

1 Peter 5:7 (King James Version)

[7]Casting all your care upon him; for he careth for you.

Psalm 50:15 (King James Version)

[15]And call upon me in the day of trouble: I will deliver thee, and thou shalt glorify me.

TIME TELLS THE TRUTH

A person's true character will show up if you give it enough time to do so.

It is important to allow time to tell you the truth before you place too much trust in the person.

Psalm 55:21 (King James Version)

[21]The words of his mouth were smoother than butter, but war was in his heart: his words were softer than oil, yet were they drawn swords.

WINDOWS OF THE MIND

Our divinely designed minds are always searching for problems in our lives that need to be solved.

This may be especially true just after a problem has been solved because our busy minds begin to look for another one to replace it with.

God told me one day to learn to minimize and maximize my thoughts according to importance just like in Microsoft Windows, and some thoughts He said should be deleted altogether.

Philippians 4:8 (King James Version)

[8]Finally, brethren, whatsoever things are true, whatsoever things are honest, whatsoever things are just, whatsoever things are pure, whatsoever things are lovely, whatsoever things are of good report; if there be any virtue, and if there be any praise, think on these

Romans 12:2 (King James Version)

^{2}And be not conformed to this world: but be ye transformed by the renewing of your mind, that ye may prove what is that good, and acceptable, and perfect, will of God.

THE CLEANSING

Un-forgiveness is as toxic to your spirit as the retaining of stool is to your body.

There will always be transgressions that need to be forgiven; therefore, forgiveness is a life-long process necessary to avoid toxicity to the spirit.

Matthew 18:21-22 (King James Version)

[21]Then came Peter to him, and said, Lord, how oft shall my brother sin against me, and I forgive him? till seven times?

[22]Jesus saith unto him, I say not unto thee, until seven times: but, until seventy times seven.

WORRY IS A BAD DINNER DATE

It is hard to enjoy the meal of the day while worrying whether there will be one on the table tomorrow.

Matthew 6:34 (King James Version)

[34]Take therefore no thought for the morrow: for the morrow shall take thought for the things of itself. .

Matthew 6:31-33 (King James Version)

[31]Therefore take no thought, saying, what shall we eat? Or, What shall we drink? Or, Wherewithal shall we be clothed?

[32](For after all these things do the Gentiles seek) for your heavenly Father knoweth that ye have need of all these things.

[33]But seek ye first the kingdom of God, and his righteousness; and all these things shall be added unto you.

WORK TO LIVE NOT TO WORK

It is good to work and to have money, but one must be careful not to let work and money have them.

One should not get so caught up in the getting that he fears spending and giving out of what he has gotten.

If one's joy in work comes only from the accumulation of money, he might as well collect brown paper bags and tin cans instead of dollars and cents because money is only paper and metal, but it is empowered by what we do with it.

It is when we use some of the money we work for to enjoy our lives or to bring joy to the lives of others, that we are working to live; otherwise, we are just living to work.

Ecclesiastes 3:13 (King James Version)

[13]And also that every man should eat and drink, and enjoy the good of all his labour, it is the gift of God

1 John 3:17 (King James Version)

[17]But whoso hath this world's good, and seeth his brother have need, and shutteth up his bowels of compassion from him, how dwelleth the love of God in him?

THE GRUDGE HOLDER

Some people hold grudges against the dead and grudges against the living until they themselves are dead. If one cannot forgive others, how can he reason that God should forgive him?

Mark 11:25 (King James Version)

25And when ye stand praying, forgive, if ye have ought against any: that your Father also which is in heaven may forgive you your trespasses.

UNHAPPY BIRTHDAYS

Oftentimes, the more birthdays one has, the more fearful they become as they approach and reach each one of them.

Some fears might be: Will I remain healthy? Will I have to go into a nursing home? Who will care for me if I cannot care for myself? Will I be a burden to my family?

In these fearful moments, one should be mindful that God has promised to continually care for His children throughout their lifetime.

God's children will never reach an age when He will say to them, "You are now grown and on your own."

He knows the number of our days and every situation and circumstance that we will encounter within those days, and He has already made provisions for our daily care even into old age.

People may wish us a happy birthday, but God wants us happy every day.

Isaiah 46:4 (New Living Translation)

[4] I will be your God throughout your lifetime until your hair is white with age. I made you, and I will care for you. I will carry you along and save you.

Psalm 37:25 (King James Version)

[25]I have been young, and now am old; yet have I not seen the righteous forsaken, nor his seed begging bread

WE NEVER GET CLOSE TO PERFECT

Life is a constant striving for perfection never to be attained, and it is only when we get close that we can see how far away we really are.

Romans 3:10 (King James Version)

[10]As it is written, There is none righteous, no, not one:

Romans 3:23 (King James Version)

[23]For all have sinned, and come short of the glory of God;

Matthew 7:3 (King James Version)

[3]And why beholdest thou the mote that is in thy brother's eye, but considerest not the beam that is in thine own eye?

SIP YOUR LIFE

Your life on this earth is like your portion of the last bottle of a fine, rare wine, so do not waste it, do not gulp it; just sip and enjoy it for once it is gone, it is gone.

James 4:14 (King James Version)

[14]Whereas ye know not what shall be on the morrow. For what is your life? It is even a vapour, that appeareth for a little time, and then vanisheth away.

COLLECT YOUR INHERITANCE

A person who has read the good news of the Bible and never claims God's promises or expects to collect on them is like an impoverished heir who wakes up every morning, and reads his rich deceased fathers will, and knows that he has been left great wealth and riches; but then puts the will back in the drawer without ever making a claim upon it and continues to live in poverty .

Ephesians 3:6 (New Living Translation)

[6] And this is God's plan: Both Gentiles and Jews who believe the Good News share equally in the riches inherited by God's children. Both are part of the same body, and both enjoy the promise of blessings because they belong to Christ Jesus

Galatians 3:29 (King James Version)

[29]And if ye be Christ's, then are ye Abraham's seed, and heirs according to the promise.

Genesis 13:2 (King James Version)

²And Abram was very rich in cattle, in silver, and in gold.

WHAT'S THE DIFFERENCE?

Is there a difference between one who believes in the existence of God but has no faith in him or his promises, and one who does not believe in the existence God?

Hebrews 11:6 (King James Version)

[6]But without faith it is impossible to please him: for he that cometh to God must believe that he is, and that he is a rewarder of them that diligently seek him.

THE MARRIAGE MOBILE

A marriage is like an automobile that you love.
It has to be tuned up and cared for routinely
regardless of low mileage or high mileage.
You have to be so tuned in to it that you can
recognize the sounds of problems and fix
them before they become larger problems. By
taking loving care of it from the very
beginning, you will not have to trade it in or
junk it.

Ephesians 5:20-21; 25-33

Giving thanks always for all things unto God
and the Father in the name of our Lord Jesus
Christ; submitting yourselves one to another
in the fear of God. Husbands, love your
wives, even as Christ also loved the church,
and gave himself for it; that he might sanctify
and cleanse it with the washing of water by
the word, that he might present it to himself a
glorious church, not having spot, or wrinkle,
or any such thing; but that it should be holy
and without blemish. So ought men to love
their wives as their own bodies. He that
loveth his wife loveth himself. For no man

ever yet hated his own flesh; but nourisheth and cherisheth it, even as the Lord the church: for we are members of his body, of his flesh, and of his bones. For this cause shall a man leave his father and mother, and shall be joined unto his wife, and they two shall be one flesh.

DEPOSIT INTO YOUR MERCY ACCOUNT

Being merciful to others is like depositing mercy into your heavenly mercy account, and when you have mercy in, you can get some mercy out when you need it.

Matthew 5:7 (King James Version)

[7]Blessed are the merciful: for they shall obtain mercy.

SHOW HIM AND HE WILL SHOW YOU

God will show you his promises. He just wants you to show Him some faith and patience.

2 Peter 1:4 (King James Version)

[4]Whereby are given unto us exceeding great and precious promises: that by these ye might be partakers of the divine nature, having escaped the corruption that is in the world through lust.

Hebrews 6:12 (King James Version)

[12]That ye be not slothful, but followers of them who through faith and patience inherit the promises.

TWO THINGS GOD TOLD ME NEVER TO FORGET

1.   Never forget who He is

Genesis 35:11 (King James Version)

[11]And God said unto him, I am God Almighty

Revelation 1:8 (King James Version)

[8]I am Alpha and Omega, the beginning and the ending, saith the Lord, which is, and which was, and which is to come, the Almighty.

2.   Never forget who I am in Christ

2 Corinthians 5:21 (King James Version)

[21]For he hath made him to be sin for us, who knew no sin; that we might be made the righteousness of God in him.

Ephesians 3:12 (New Living Translation)

[12] Because of Christ and our faith in him,[a] we can now come boldly and confidently into God's presence.

Galatians 4: 7 (King James Version)

[7]Wherefore thou art no more a servant, but a son; and if a son, then an heir of God through Christ

Philippians 4:13 (King James Version)

[13]I can do all things through Christ which strengthened me.

FOR ONE THING OR ANOTHER

One will never reach a point in life when he becomes so self- sufficient in all areas of his life that he won't need God for anything.

A person may not know that they need Him, acknowledge that they need Him, or even ask for His help when they know that they need Him, but that person without a doubt, will always need Him.

John 16:33 (King James Version)

[33]These things I have spoken unto you, that in me ye might have peace. In the world ye shall have tribulation: but be of good cheer; I have overcome the world.

THE RULES OF GOD'S ROAD

If after asking God to direct your path, it seems like your life is at a standstill or you're stuck in a traffic jam, do not despair. You can be assured that your life is moving in God's divine order because God has set the speed limit on the path of your life.

He has placed the stop signs and speed bumps just where He wants them. He has set up construction zones and road blocks to redirect you and is controlling all of the traffic lights.

And even though you may break His rules of the road, He will never revoke your license to drive. You will always have the free will to make your own choices and drive your own life even if you choose to drive it into a ditch without His direction.

Proverbs 3:5-6 (King James Version)

[5]Trust in the LORD with all thine heart; and lean not unto thine own understanding.

⁶In all thy ways acknowledge him, and he shall direct thy paths.

Psalm 16:11 (King James Version)

¹¹Thou wilt shew me the path of life: in thy presence is fulness of joy; at thy right hand there are pleasures for evermore.

HOME SCHOOLING

There are no perfect children because we live in an imperfect world with imperfect influences and some good but imperfect parents.

Our children will make mistakes, but for parents to calmly deal with those mistakes, they may need to think back to the mistakes they made in their youth.

In this world, more than ever, our children are being taught that much of the good their parents taught them is now bad and much of the bad parents warned them against is now good and acceptable. Some of their teachers are: the internet, music, videos, television, magazines, radio, their peers; and their influence on our children can be life-changing.

Parents should teach their children that even though they one day will no longer be under their parental, they will always be under the higher authority of God.

They should be taught that God is forgiving, but that sin has consequences, and they will have to live with the consequences of their life's choices.

They should be taught the totality of God's unconditional love for them in such a way as to create in them a love for God so sincere that their desire to please Him will be stronger than their desire to please themselves. This desire to please God will positively influence their friendships, mate selections, and all of the choices they make as adults.

Proverbs 22:6 (King James Version)

⁶Train up a child in the way he should go: and when he is old, he will not depart from it.

Deuteronomy 6:5-7 (King James Version)

⁵And thou shalt love the LORD thy God with all thine heart, and with all thy soul, and with all thy might.

⁶And these words, which I command thee this day, shall be in thine heart:

⁷And thou shalt teach them diligently unto thy children, and shalt talk of them when thou sittest in thine house, and when thou walkest by the way, and when thou liest down, and when thou risest up.

GOD'S BABY SHOWER

God had what we might liken unto a baby shower for every child that has ever been born into this world.

The date of the shower was at creation,; the time was before the child was placed in his mother's womb; and the only three attendees were The Father God, The Son Jesus and The Holy Spirit.

The gifts that were showered upon the child by the three in attendance, encompassed everything that each child would ever need throughout their entire life.

Psalm 22:9-10 (New Living Translation)

[9] Yet you brought me safely from my mother's womb
and led me to trust you at my mother's breast.
[10] I was thrust into your arms at my birth.
You have been my God from the moment I was born.

Jeremiah 1:5 (King James Version)

⁵Before I formed thee in the belly I knew thee; and before thou camest forth out of the womb I sanctified thee

Philippians 4:19 (King James Version)

¹⁹But my God shall supply all your need according to his riches in glory by Christ Jesus.

KEEP YOUR GPS ON
(GOD'S POSITIONING SYSTEM)

When God is the driving force in your life, you may not know the way he will take, but you should know that He will get you safely where He wants you to go. You should be able to trust God to direct your path of life more than you trust your GPS (Global Positioning System) system to direct your path on the road. God sits higher than the satllites of your GPS; your connection to Him will never be lost, and He will never have to say RECALCULATIING

Job 28:24 (King James Version)

²⁴For he looketh to the ends of the earth, and seeth under the whole heaven;

100

THE SIMPLICITY OF SALVATION

God's plan for man's salvation, which is to pass from death unto eternal life with Him, is so simple and yet so profound.

Salvation is not something that we can earn. We can never be good enough to earn a place in heaven or pay enough tithes and offerings to buy access.

God made salvation both free and simple because He did not want anyone to miss it.

Jesus through his death on the cross took the punishment from God for every sin we have committed and every sin we will commit, and salvation is ours simply by believing and confessing that this is so. Yes, it is as simple as believing in the death, burial and resurrection and deity of Jesus Christ.

And yes, we can believe and continue to sin, ask and be forgiven and still go to heaven in the afterlife, but all sin has consequences within this life.

Once we fully realize how much God loves us by sending His only son to die instead of us and to provide us with direct access to Him 24/7 (His line is never busy, and He has an infinite calling plan), it becomes easy to love God back. The more we love Him, the more we will want to obey Him, to please Him, to serve Him and converse with Him.

It is within the development of this personal and intimate relationship and love of God that we can   find true love, peace, joy, victory, happiness, and everything we need for life and above all eternal life with God.

Romans 10:9-10

That if thou shalt confess with thy mouth the Lord Jesus, and shalt believe in thine heart that God hath raised him from the dead, thou shalt be saved. For with the heart man believeth unto righteousness; and with the mouth confession is made unto salvation.

John 3:16 (King James Version)

[16]For God so loved the world that he gave his only begotten Son, that whosoever believeth in him should not perish, but have everlasting life.

LONG DISTANCE LOVING

It is a good thing to stay far away from bad influences even if they are close relatives or friends. You can still love them, but there are some people you have to love from a distance.

Proverbs 22:5 (New King James Version)

5 Thorns *and* snares *are* in the way of the perverse;
He who guards his soul will be far from them.

1 Corinthians 15:33 (New Living Translation)

33 "bad company corrupts good character."

MEASURING SUCCESS

One should not measure success by that of others or in dollars and cents.

Success should be measured by the amount of joy and happiness your work or enterprise contributes to your life.

1 Timothy 6:6 (New Living Translation)

[6] Yet true godliness with contentment is itself great wealth.

Ecclesiastes 4:6 King James Bible

Better is an handful with quietness, than both the hands full with travail and vexation of spirit.

GOD DOES NOT WANT YOU TO BE POOR

The poor cannot do the will of God and help the poor if they themselves are poor. God did not plan for His children to be poor. His plans and promises are for our provisions and wealth and not for our poverty.

Psalm 112:1-3 (New Living Translation)

[1] Praise the LORD!

How joyful are those who fear the LORD
and delight in obeying his commands.
[2] Their children will be successful everywhere;
an entire generation of godly people will be blessed.
[3] They themselves will be wealthy,
and their good deeds will last forever.

Proverbs 10:22 (New Living Translation)

[22] The blessing of the LORD makes a person rich,
and he adds no sorrow with it.

2 Corinthians 8:9

(New Living Translation)

⁹ You know the generous grace of our Lord Jesus Christ. Though he was rich, yet for your sakes he became poor, so that by his poverty he could make you rich.

2 Corinthians 9:8 (King James Version)

⁸And God is able to make all grace abound toward you; that ye, always having all sufficiency in all things, may abound to every good work

PERCEPTION

Do not say: every time I get some money I
have to spend it on something that I need.
Say: every time I need some money I get it.

Philippians 4:19 (King James Version)

[19]But my God shall supply all your need
according to his riches in glory by Christ
Jesus.

SEEING IS NOT BELIEVING

Mankind says seeing is believing, but God
says believing is seeing.

Mark 9:23 (King James Version)

[23]Jesus said unto him, If thou canst believe, all
things are possible to him that believeth.

TELL THE TRUTH BUT...

One should always tell the truth but the truth should not always be told.

Proverbs 11:13 (King James Version)

[13]A talebearer revealeth secrets: but he that is of a faithful spirit concealeth the matter

LESSONS OF LIFE

We should not beat ourselves up over the mistakes we have made in life; rather, we should learn good lessons from them. If we had been born perfect, we would be God incarnate; but we were born imperfect, and we are us. We are the sum of the lessons learned from our experiences, and if we learn good lessons, we become good human beings.

Philippians 3:13 (King James Version)

[13]Brethren, I count not myself to have apprehended: but this one thing I do, forgetting those things which are behind, and reaching forth unto those things which are before,

Romans 3:23 (King James Version)

[23]For all have sinned, and come short of the glory of God;

NO VIPS WITH GOD

Whether you are rich, poor, uneducated, well-educated or somewhere in between; whether you are the pastor of a mega church or just a member, whatever your ethnicity or stature in life, God does not esteem one of His children above another. God loves us all equally; we all have the same access to Him and His undivided attention. We are equal heirs to His promises.

Acts 10:34 (King James Version)

[34]Then Peter opened his mouth, and said, Of a truth I perceive that God is no respecter of persons:

THE TONGUE FIGHT

Learning to control one's tongue can be the difference between life and death.

If someone throws a verbal pebble at you, you do not have to throw a verbal brick back at them.

Proverbs 18:21 (King James Version)

[21]Death and life are in the power of the tongue: and they that love it shall eat the fruit thereof.

Proverbs 15:1 (King James Version)

[1]A soft answer turneth away wrath: but grievous words stir up anger.

James 1:19 (New Living Translation)

[19] Understand this, my dear brothers and sisters: You must all be quick to listen, slow to speak, and slow to get angry.

HEALING OR REVEALING

There are times when we are praying for our body's healing when all that is needed is a revealing of what we may be doing to our bodies that is causing it to need healing.

In answer to our prayer for healing, God will sometimes provide us with a revealing of what we are doing that is harmful to our bodies. We often change medications when all that is needed is a change in lifestyle.

After we make the revealed and necessary changes, our body can then begin to heal itself just as it was created by God to do.

Jeremiah 33:6 (King James Version)

⁶Behold, I will bring it health and cure, and I will cure them, and will reveal unto them the abundance of peace and truth.

GOD HEARD YOU BEFORE YOU

Just as God at creation preordained the sun to rise and set and the seasons to change, He also preordained our every prayer to be answered, our every need to be met, and He factored these answers and needs into all that He created.

For instance, God heard the prayers of those needing or desiring to fly off to some distant place before they were born.

He, therefore, provided the prototype in the bird, placed the idea for the airplane in the mind of man, and had already provided in creation the natural resources for its development.

God wants us to expect answers to prayers and needs to be met with the same faithful expectation we have of the sun rising and setting and the seasons changing because both have been preordained by the same infallible spoken word of God.

Isaiah 65:24 (King James Version)

²⁴And it shall come to pass, that before they call, I will answer

Isaiah 55:10-11 (King James Version)

¹⁰For as the rain cometh down, and the snow from heaven, and returneth not thither, but watereth the earth, and maketh it bring forth and bud, that it may give seed to the sower, and bread to the eater:

¹¹So shall my word be that goeth forth out of my mouth: it shall not return unto me void, but it shall accomplish that which I please, and it shall prosper in the thing whereto I sent it.

THE DIVINE RECIPE FOR EVERYTHING

How great is God?

It is impossible for Mankind to fully comprehend the awesomeness, the greatness, and the power of the almighty God.

Everything that mankind has ever created was first created by God.

Man created a light bulb, but God created light. Every painting of anything is only a copy or God's original.

Hebrews 3:4 (King James Version)

[4]For every house is builded by some man; but he that built all things is God.

Nehemiah 9:6 (King James Version)

[6]Thou, even thou, art LORD alone; thou hast made heaven, the heaven of heavens, with their entire host, the earth, and all things that are therein, the seas, and all that is therein, and thou preservest them all; and the host of heaven worshippeth thee.

Psalm 19:1 (New Living Translation)

[1] The heavens proclaim the glory of God.
The skies display his craftsmanship.

FRIENDS FOR A REASON AND A SEASON

There are times when a friend is no longer a friend, or contact is lost with someone who had been an important part of one's life.

It is important to understand that God sends people in and out of our lives for reasons and for seasons to accomplish His purposes.

Once their purposes are accomplished, He may send these laborers in another direction to another life and for other purposes.

Ecclesiastes 3:1 (King James Version)

[1]To every thing there is a season, and a time to every purpose under the heaven:

LOVE YOUR NEIGHBOR BUT DON'T FORGET YOURSELF

The Bible teaches us that we are to love our neighbor as ourselves.

From this command, we know that God expects us to love ourselves.

We are to love ourselves in the same way that God loves us, which is unconditionally, and that is the way He expects us to love our neighbors.

Mark 12:30-31 (King James Version)

[30]And thou shalt love the Lord thy God with all thy heart, and with all thy soul, and with all thy mind, and with all thy strength: this is the first commandment.

[31]And the second is like, namely this, Thou shalt love thy neighbour as thyself. There is none other commandment greater than these.

1 Corinthians 13-4

[1] If I could speak all the languages of earth and of angels, but didn't love others, I would

only be a noisy gong or a clanging cymbal. [2] If I had the gift of prophecy, and if I understood all of God's secret plans and possessed all knowledge, and if I had such faith that I could move mountains, but didn't love others, I would be nothing. [3] If I gave everything I have to the poor and even sacrificed my body, I could boast about it; [a] but if I didn't love others, I would have gained nothing.

[4] Love is patient and kind. Love is not jealous or boastful or proud [5] or rude. It does not demand its own way. It is not irritable, and it keeps no record of being wronged. [6] It does not rejoice about injustice but rejoices whenever the truth wins out. [7] Love never gives up, never loses faith, is always hopeful, and endures through every circumstance.

LIFE HAS MANY TEACHERS

From a fool one can learn the dangers of foolishness and from the wise the value of wisdom. Everyone's life can teach us something.

We don't have to experience the bad if we can learn good lessons from the lives of both the wise and the foolish.

1 Corinthians 10:11 (King James Version)

[11]Now all these things happened unto them for examples: and they are written for our admonition

WHOM WOULD YOU NOT WANT TO SEE IN HEAVEN?

If there are people you hate so much or have so much unforgiveness for that you would not want to see them in heaven if you got there, you may be placing yourself in danger of getting there.

Matthew 6:15 (King James Version)

[15]But if ye forgive not men their trespasses, neither will your Father forgive your trespasses.

THE REPETITIOUS PRAYER

I was praying to God one night, and shortly after I started, God said to me, "I heard that already. Is there anything new?"

I then realized that what I was praying about were things that I had already prayed about many times before. God said to me that He heard all of those prayers and was answering them, and if there were no new problems, then I had nothing to worry about.

I knew then that what God wanted from me was thankfulness and praise for what he has done and for what I expect Him to do.

Matthew 6:7 (King James Version)

[7]But when ye pray, use not vain repetitions, as the heathen do: for they think that they shall be heard for their much speaking.

Psalm 100:4 (King James Version)

[4]Enter into his gates with thanksgiving, and into his courts with praise: be thankful unto him, and bless his name.

1 John 5:14-15 (King James Version)

[14]And this is the confidence that we have in him, that, if we ask any thing according to his will, he heareth us:

[15]And if we know that he hear us, whatsoever we ask, we know that we have the petitions that we desired of him.

HOW? WHEN? WHAT? WHERE? GOD

If anxiety sets in while waiting on God and one begins to wonder how, when, where, and what God is going to do, faith can answer the questions.

The How is by using His omnipotent power; the When is within His divine order; the What is whatever needs to be done; and the Where is of His divine choosing.

After faith answers the questions, the only thing left for us to do is the praise Him.

Philippians 4:6-7 (New King James Version)

[6] Be anxious for nothing, but in everything by prayer and supplication, with thanksgiving, let your requests be made known to God; [7] and the peace of God, which surpasses all understanding, will guard your hearts and minds through Christ Jesus.

Genesis 18:14 (King James Version)

[14] Is any thing too hard for the LORD?

THE THOUGHT THIEF

Do not allow bad thoughts to steal the joy from a good day. On a bad day, think about a good day!

Philippians 4:8 (King James Version)

[8]Finally, brethren, whatsoever things are true, whatsoever things are honest, whatsoever things are just, whatsoever things are pure, whatsoever things are lovely, whatsoever things are of good report; if there be any virtue, and if there be any praise, think on these things.

TIT FOR TAT

When the devil tries to condemn you through your thoughts by bringing up your God forgiven and forgotten past, tell the devil about his future.

Revelation 20:10 (King James Version)

[10]And the devil that deceived them was cast into the lake of fire and brimstone, where the beast and the false prophet are, and shall be tormented day and night for ever and ever.

James 4:7 (King James Version)

[7]Submit yourselves therefore to God. Resist the devil, and he will flee from you

John 3:17 (New King James Version)

[17] For God did not send His Son into the world to condemn the world, but that the world through Him might be saved.

WHAT GOD WILL NOT REMEMBER

Although you and others may remember your forgiven sins, you can be comforted by knowing that what really matters is that God has chosen not to remember them.

Jesus' death on the cross provided us with forgiveness for all of our sins.

While it is hard for us as well as for others to forgive or forget our transgressions, we should know that what God has forgiven, he has also chosen to forget.

Hebrews 8:12 (King James Version)

[12]For I will be merciful to their unrighteousness, and their sins and their iniquities will I remember no more.

Isaiah 1:18 (King James Version)

[18]Come now, and let us reason together, saith the LORD: though your sins be as scarlet, they shall be as white as snow

ANOTHER WAY TO LOOK AT IT

If you cannot think of any good things that have happened in your life to thank God for, thank Him for some bad things that did not happen to you.

1 Thessalonians 5:18 (King James Version)

[18]In every thing give thanks: for this is the will of God in Christ Jesus concerning you.

THE EMOTIONS CONTROLLER

The consequences of uncontrolled emotions are many; they have resulted in divorce, murder, imprisonment and death.

One episode of uncontrolled emotions has caused many good people to be in bad situations. Some to be imprisoned for life for doing things they and others would never have believed possible for them to have done.

When one, however, is filled with The Holy Spirit of God, he yields his spirit to God's spirit and become one with Him; consequently, what is manifested in his emotions is not the fruit of his own spirit but the fruit of God's spirit that is love, joy, peace, longsuffering, gentleness, goodness, faith, meekness and temperance.

1 Corinthians 6:17 (King James Version)

[17]But he that is joined unto the Lord is one spirit.

Galatians 5:16 (King James Version)

[16]This I say then, Walk in the Spirit, and ye shall not fulfill the lust of the flesh.

Galatians 5:22-23 (King James Version)

[22]But the fruit of the Spirit is love, joy, peace, longsuffering, gentleness, goodness, faith, [23]Meekness, temperance:

THE ULTIMATE LACK OF FAITH

Suicide is a demonstration of the ultimate lack of faith in God Almighty.

It is the intentional destruction of the body that is the home of the Holy Spirit of God.

Every gift of life is for a reason and a season, all of which has been predetermined by God. We did not determine the day of our birth and have not been given the authority to determine the day of our death.

To commit suicide is to say to God, who created the heavens and the earth with His spoken word and sent His only son to die so that we might have eternal life, "You don't have enough power or enough love for me to solve my problems".

Rather than one taking their own life, they should place anything, everything and any situation that would cause them to even think about committing suicide in the hands of God.

With just the faith of a little grain of mustard seed, one can summon all the powers of God to work on their behalf to move mountains and turn their darkest nights into bright days and their days into years filled with blessings that were preordained to arrive in God's divine order in the fullness of their lifetime.

1 Corinthians 6:19-20 (New Living Translation)

[19] Don't you realize that your body is the temple of the Holy Spirit, who lives in you and was given to you by God? You do not belong to yourself, [20] for God bought you with a high price. So you must honor God with your body.

Ephesians 5:29 (King James Version)

[29]For no man ever yet hated his own flesh; but nourisheth and cherisheth it, even as the Lord the church:

Luke 17:6 (New Living Translation)

6 The Lord answered, "If you have faith even as small as a mustard seed, you could say to this mulberry tree, 'May you be uprooted and thrown into the sea and it would obey you!

Ecclesiastes 3:1-2 (New Living Translation)

A Time for Everything

¹ For everything there is a season,
a time for every activity under heaven.
² A time to be born and a time to die.

John 16:33 (New Living Translation)

³³ I have told you all this so that you may have peace in me. Here on earth you will have many trials and sorrows. But take heart, because I have overcome the world."

Psalm 50:15 (New Living Translation)

¹⁵ Then call on me when you are in trouble,
and I will rescue you,
and you will give me glory

UNMERITED FAVOR

When good things happen in our lives, we often times try to relate it to something good we may have done to justify the blessing.

If God rewarded us only when we did something good, He would have to take something away whenever we did something bad.

What we experience everyday of our lives is God's unmerited favor, and just as we would do when accepting any gift, we need to say "Thank you."

Psalm 103:10-14 (New Living Translation)

¹⁰ He does not punish us for all our sins;
  he does not deal harshly with us, as we
       deserve.
¹¹ For his unfailing love toward those who
       fear him
  is as great as the height of the heavens
       above the earth.
¹² He has removed our sins as far from us
  as the east is from the west.
¹³ The LORD is like a father to his children,

135

tender and compassionate to those who
fear him.
¹⁴ For he knows how weak we are;
he remembers we are only dust.

Psalm 136 (King James Version)

¹O give thanks unto the LORD; for he is
good: for his mercy endureth for ever

NAME YOUR OWN HOLIDAY

One should not save the best of what he has for an established holiday or what might be considered a special occasion.

Every day of life is holiday, and all one has to do is give it a name and enjoy it.

Psalm 118:24 (King James Version)

[24]This is the day which the LORD hath made; we will rejoice and be glad in it.

Ecclesiastes 5:18 (King James Version)

[18]Behold that which I have seen: it is good and comely for one to eat and to drink, and to enjoy the good of all his labour that he taketh under the sun all the days of his life, which God giveth him: for it is his portion.

YOU HAVE WHAT YOU NEED
TO GET WHAT YOU WANT

Through the power of The Holy Spirit, Christians can have and do   immeasurably more than they think they can.

The power of The Holy Spirit works through faith, and the good news is that God has already given us the amount of faith we need for the power of The Holy Spirit to work on our behalf.

All we need is faith in the power of The Holy Spirit, faith that The Holy Spirit is within us and faith that God has already given us the faith we need for the power to work.

Through this trinity of faith, we can see the work of The Holy Spirit manifested victoriously in our every need, desire and in every aspect of our lives.

Acts 1:8 (King James Version)

[8]But ye shall receive power, after that the Holy Ghost is come upon you

1 Corinthians 3:16 (King James Version)

[16]Know ye not that ye are the temple of God, and that the Spirit of God dwelleth in you?

Romans 12:3 (King James Version)

God hath dealt to every man the measure of faith

Ephesians 3:20 (King James Version)

[20]Now unto him that is able to do exceeding abundantly above all that we ask or think, according to the power that worketh in us,

FOLLOWING THE LEADER

Be careful where you let your mind wander because your actions may want to follow.

James 1:14-15 (King James Version)

[14]But every man is tempted, when he is drawn away of his own lust, and enticed.

[15]Then when lust hath conceived, it bringeth forth sin: and sin, when it is finished, bringeth forth death.

2 Corinthians 10:5 (King James Version)

[5]Casting down imaginations, and every high thing that exalteth itself against the knowledge of God, and bringing into captivity every thought to the obedience of Christ

FROM FOE TO FRIEND

It is wise to pray for your enemies. Their change of heart and character will not only be a blessing for them but for you because you may lose an enemy and find a friend.

Luke 6:27-28 (King James Version)

[27]But I say unto you which hear, Love your enemies, do good to them which hate you,

[28]Bless them that curse you, and pray for them which despitefully use you.

WHEN GOD SAYS NO

When it seems like God has said no to your petitions, you should know that He has really said yes to His better plan for your life.

Making Him Lord of your life gives Him the authority to overrule your plans in lieu of His better plans and yields your will to His will.

Once you become fully persuaded of God's love for you and that He has everything in divine order and working towards your best interest, then when He says no, you may not understand it; but you will be just as happy as when He says yes.

Proverbs 16:1 (New Living Translation)

[1] We can make our own plans,
but the LORD gives the right answer.

Jeremiah 29:11 (King James Version)

[11]For I know the thoughts that I think toward you, saith the LORD, thoughts of peace, and not of evil, to give you an expected end.

Romans 8:28 (King James Version)

[28]And we know that all things work together for good to them that love God, to them who are the called according to his purpose.

NO COMPARISON

The validation of mankind's love by a hug a kiss, a touch or the words "I Do" cannot compare with how God validated His love for us in John 3:16.

John 3:16 (King James Version)

[16]For God so loved the world that he gave his only begotten Son, that whosoever believeth in him should not perish, but have everlasting life.

John 15:13 (King James Version)

[13]Greater love hath no man than this, that a man lay down his life for his friends

GET OUT OF LIFE ALIVE

By seeking to love, laugh, and enjoy the gift of life throughout one's lifetime up to and including the day he passes from this life into eternal life, one will have gotten out of life alive.

John 10:10 (Amplified Bible)

[10]The thief comes only in order to steal and kill and destroy. I came that they may have and enjoy life, and have it in abundance (to the full, till it [a]overflows).

John 11:26 (King James Version)

[26]And whosoever liveth and believeth in me shall never die

HOLIER THAN THOU

Because one prays more, reads the Bible more, quotes scripture and verse more, attends church more or gives more in church offerings does that make him more righteous than another?

The standard for righteousness was set by Jesus Christ, and no man can measure up to His standard.

We have, therefore, been made righteous in the eyes of God, simply by believing in the only righteous one, Jesus Christ.

2 Corinthians 5:21 (King James Version)

²¹For he hath made him to be sin for us, who knew no sin; that we might be made the righteousness of God in him.

Romans 3:10 (King James Version)

¹⁰As it is written, There is none righteous, no, not one:

Ephesians 2:8 (King James Version)

[8]For by grace are ye saved through faith; and that not of yourselves: it is the gift of God:

THE SALUTATION TO LIFE

It has been said that one should try to live each day of life as though it is his last.

On your last day, however, you would be rushing to do things that you may have always wanted to do and did not . There would be sadness in having to say "goodbye".

If, however, you seek to live each day of life as though it is your first day, there would be joy and excitement because you would be saying "hello" to life and all of it's possibilities.

Psalm 118:24 (King James Version)

[24]This is the day which the LORD hath made; we will rejoice and be glad in it.

YOU, THE LIFE CHANGER

You can change your life simply by changing your mind.

Proverbs 23:7 (King James Version)

[7]For as he thinketh in his heart, so is he

THE HEALER

God may heal through miracles, and God may heal through medicine; however, God chooses to heal. He is always the healer.

Psalm 103:2-3 (King James Version)

[2]Bless the LORD, O my soul, and forget not all his benefits:

[3]Who forgiveth all thine iniquities; who healeth all thy diseases

Revelation 22:2 (King James Version)

and the leaves of the tree were for the healing of the nations

DON'T LOSE YOURSELF

If you hate someone because he hates you or tries to get back at someone by doing likewise to him, you lost and he won. You lost yourself, and he won you over because you became like him.

Romans 12:21 (King James Version)

[21]Be not overcome of evil, but overcome evil with good

FAMILY AFFAIRS

The challenges of having a large family are often like having a part- time job added to your already busy life.

The good thing, however, is that it can pay full time benefits.

Proverbs 17:17 (New Living Translation)

[17] a brother is born to help in time of need.

Galatians 6:9 (King James Version)

[9]And let us not be weary in well doing: for in due season we shall reap, if we faint not

DON'T BE CHOSEN

Be careful who you let into your life and your confidence. It's easier to let them in than it is to get them out. Choose your friends; and do not let them choose you.

Proverbs 12:26 (New King James Version)

26 The righteous should choose his friends carefully,
For the way of the wicked leads them astray

Proverbs 13:20 (New King James Version)

20 He who walks with wise *men* will be wise,
But the companion of fools will be destroyed.

1 Corinthians 15:33 (New Living Translation)

33 "bad company corrupts good character."

DON'T MAKE A U-TURN

Waiting on God may sometimes seem like being in a car that has been stopped by a slow train at a railroad crossing.

You know that your blessings are on the other side, but you get tired of waiting and just want to get moving. So you impulsively make a u-turn to try a different route even though you do not know where it will lead.

While traveling the new route with no directions, you end up encountering even more obstacles, and it takes much longer for you to get to your blessings than if you had waited on the train to pass.

After asking God for direction in any situation, He will place you on the right path, and it is important for you to stay on that path.

God knew beforehand everything that would be on the path He placed you on. He knew everything that would slow you down and speed you up, but all has been timed to move within His divine order.

Psalm 27:14 (King James Version)

[14]Wait on the LORD: be of good courage, and he shall strengthen thine heart: wait, I say, on the LORD.

Romans 8:28 (King James Version)

[28]And we know that all things work together for good to them that love God, to them who are the called according to his purpose.

HEART TO HEART

When you really want to get your point across to someone, always speak from the heart because when you speak from the heart, you will speak to the heart of the other person.

Luke 6:45 (King James Version)

[45]A good man out of the good treasure of his heart bringeth forth that which is good; and an evil man out of the evil treasure of his heart bringeth forth that which is evil: for of the abundance of the heart his mouth speaketh.

THE SCHOOL OF LIFE

Life is your school; you must attend its class every day. You cannot master it, as there are no Masters or any other degrees that you can earn.

When The Holy Spirit in you is the teacher, however, you will find joy in His class; and His curriculum will come from one book - the Bible.

God sent Jesus to take all of your tests, and even though He was the one who took and passed them, God will turn to you one day and say "well done my child, pass on to eternal life"

John 14:26 (King James Version)

[26]But the Comforter, which is the Holy Ghost, whom the Father will send in my name, he shall teach you all things, and bring all things to your remembrance, whatsoever I have said unto you.

2 Timothy 3:16-17 (New Living Translation)

¹⁶ All Scripture is inspired by God and is useful to teach us what is true and to make us realize what is wrong in our lives. It corrects us when we are wrong and teaches us to do what is right. ¹⁷ God uses it to prepare and equip his people to do every good work

Ephesians 2:8-9 (King James Version)

⁸For by grace are ye saved through faith; and that not of yourselves: it is the gift of God:

⁹Not of works, lest any man should boast

THE MARRIAGE REHEARSAL

When two people decide to live together before marriage and they have a serious argument, the first thought of one or the other might be, "I'm not married to this person, I'm going to just pack up and leave."

When one is married, however, that same argument might be followed by a more thoughtful process that involves considering the complexity and consequences of the dissolution of marriage. Instead of his first thought being I'm going to just pack up and leave,   he or she may more likely reason that it is better to try to work the problems out and stay together.

Trial-runs gone badly have caused many to run away from what could have been a good and lasting marriage.

2 Timothy 2:22 (King James Version)

[22]Flee also youthful lusts: but follow righteousness, faith, charity, peace, with them that call on the Lord out of a pure heart.

159

Proverbs 18:22 (King James Version)

[22]Whoso findeth a wife findeth a good thing, and obtaineth favour of the LORD.

THE PLEASER

Trying to please everyone is like decorating your house with things that you hate to please your visitors and then having to live in it by yourself.

Galatians 1:10 (King James Version)

[10]For do I now persuade men, or God? or do I seek to please men? for if I yet pleased men, I should not be the servant of Christ.

THE POWER WORD

"No" is the most powerful word in all languages. "No" will keep you out of all the trouble that "yes" can get you into, but only if you have the courage to say it and mean it when you do.

Matthew 5:37 (Amplified Bible)

[37]Let your Yes be simply Yes, and your No be simply No

THE HAPPINESS KEEPER

The natural desire of every human being is to be happy.

One's search for happiness, however, usually begins with people, places and things; but happiness that comes from these cannot be sustained because people change, places are sometimes out of reach and things break.

Happiness cannot be sustained by anything that is without and destructible; it must be sustained from that which is within and is indestructible.

The Holy Spirit is the indestructible sustainer of happiness, and His desire is to live within us.

The Holy Spirit is ours for the asking, and He does not turn down any invitation.

When invited in, He never comes empty-handed but generously brings gifts, and fruits of love, peace, joy and all of the power of God to work on our behalf.

The Holy Spirit does not change, is never out of reach, and cannot be destroyed.

When our happiness comes from the indwelling of The Holy Spirit, it can be sustained within any condition, situation, or circumstance by our faith that He will cause all things to work together for our good.

Ecclesiastes 5:10 (King James Version)

[10]He that loveth silver shall not be satisfied with silver; nor he that loveth abundance with increase

Galatians 5:22 (King James Version)

[22]But the fruit of the Spirit is love, joy, peace, longsuffering, gentleness, goodness, faith